BIG
GIRL
PANTS

A Women's Guide to Strutting Toward the Life She Craves

LISA BAIRD PANOS

COPYRIGHT

DISCLAIMER

Cover Design: MadHat Books
Editing: Lindsay Fischer and Amy Brooks

DEDICATION

To Hannah and Caroline Panos:
May you, my two beautiful daughters, always follow your
hearts and dreams and create lives *you* absolutely love.

To Nick Baird:
Thanks for the words you wrote in my 18th birthday card;
they have propelled me through life:
"Be what you want to be. Do what you want to do. You
have my utmost confidence and respect. Go for it." -Dad

To Veronica Baird (Babby):
Thanks for always being true to who you are and for
teaching me it's okay to do the same.
This life lesson has been simply priceless, mama bear.

To Phil Hoey:
Thanks for being my safe place since the first moment I
met you. And thank you for always supporting me on all
my crazy ventures.

TABLE OF CONTENTS

PREFACE

"Put on your big girl pants."

If you're a woman in the western world, it's likely someone has said this to or around you. A colloquialism, people easily interpret these six words because they're subconsciously trained to know the meaning without anyone having to say what they're intending to say.

So, what does the phrase mean?

Deal with it.
Get over it.
Suck it up.
Grow up.
Take a risk.
Follow through.

And while we've all heard it at some point, it's rare to be encouraged by someone using this phrase. Because no one ever tells us *how*, do they? They just expect us to stop doing whatever they feel is inappropriate or unappealing and instantaneously see another way.

I don't know about you, but when my life gets hard, I don't want someone to tell me to suck it up. I want compassion and understanding. I want help. I want to learn how to be whole again, how to move forward, and *how* to put on my big girl pants.

INTRODUCTION

HOW THE HELL DID I END UP HERE?

You have done everything right: you went to college, started a career and got married. You bought a suburban house with a white-picket fence and had as many kids as you wanted. You do yoga, occasionally contribute to your emergency fund and, for the most part, live a balanced life.

All the milestones have been checked off, yet your life feels like a total and complete snooze-fest (like the kale you eat) because you do the same thing day in and day out.

On Tuesday afternoons, you work from home but find yourself roaming through Target, gabbing on the phone with your best friend, and filling your shopping cart with yellow highlighters, cat toys, peanut M&Ms, and about $200 worth of other crap you don't need.

Running late to pick up your kids, you hurry to get a good spot in the *stop, drop, and go* line. You notice other mothers walking to greet their little darlings at the classroom doors and think, *who has time to park their car, stroll up to the school and make idle chit chat with the other moms?* As you wait in your air-conditioned SUV, you read through your missed emails, thinking about everywhere you are behind, at work and home.

You can't win.

Finally, you get the kids home and scramble to make a healthy snack, only to realize you forgot to buy milk and carrots. The *ding* on your cell phone alerts you that your husband will be home late (again), and just when you think your plate can't get any fuller, your boss calls and says he needs you to send your edits to the magazine publisher. Ahem, tonight.

Is this my life? you think. *How do I have everything I thought I wanted yet feel so lonely, exhausted and unfulfilled?* Your shoulders are so tight they hit your gold hoop earrings. *Breathe. This isn't that bad*, you try to convince yourself. *I shouldn't complain. I am lucky and blessed. I have everything I have ever wanted.*

Hours later, when the kids are in bed, the dishes are in the dishwasher, and you've finally made the necessary edits for your boss, you pour yourself a glass of Cabernet Sauvignon and enjoy the quiet of the house, plopping down on the couch, and scrolling through your Facebook newsfeed. Your mind wanders as you peer through everyone else's posts:

I wish I had her life. She and her husband are still so in love. They always go out to dinner and concerts together— even during the week. My husband and I barely look at each other anymore.

I wish I could work from home every day like she does. I can't believe she left her corporate job to start her own business. I'd love to set my own schedule. I hate having a boss who questions my every move.

Does she even eat? She is so slim and fit. I bet she works out all the time. I wish I could squeeze my fat butt into that dress.

How does she afford to travel all the time? She has four daughters, for God's sake. Four tuitions and four weddings. She must have family money.

And so on and so forth.

You know the routine: you start down your dead-end path of comparison and jealousy, wondering why everyone besides you has it all. Before you know it, you find yourself pouring your second glass of wine (this time to the rim) and dreaming about the life you wish you had:

- A rewarding career
- A hot body
- Greater passion with your spouse (or any passion, for that matter)
- A travel fund
- Closer friendships
- More freedom in your schedule

- Better communication with your teenagers
- Etcetera, etcetera, etcetera.

It all sounds so wonderful, you think. Except your inner mean girl (that bitch) keeps piping in, coming up with a plethora of reasons why you can't have these things:

I don't have enough time.
I don't have enough money.
I can't.
I shouldn't.
I'm too tired.
I'm too scared.
I'm not good enough.
I'm not smart, worthy, pretty, or thin enough.

Thus, the cycle continues.

Dream. Excuse. Dream. Excuse. Dream. Excuse.

Perhaps you have a few excuses as to why you aren't living a life you love. You aren't alone. Many women have reasons they feel stuck in ho-hum routines. But, guess what? You are not stuck, even if you think you are.

Want a new job? You can get one.

How about a better relationship with your partner? You can have that too.

A hot-fudge sundae (even though you are on a diet)? All yours.

Let me repeat the critically important message you must understand from this point on:

YOU ARE NOT STUCK.

Ladies, you are the authors of your lives and can create soul-on-fire stories. This book was designed to help you find your own secret to happiness and a kick-ass life. But first, you must understand the journey can only begin when you stop looking outside of yourself for answers and start truly listening to the voice within.

Truth time? This voyage is tricky and—if you do the work—you'll be checking in with yourself constantly, even as you grow and evolve. Don't let that be a deterrent, please. It's the most rewarding, bravest move you can make for yourself. Case in point, it took me a year to get up the courage to write this book even though I know the usual hiccups and places women stop pursuing dreams. I still struggled because of excuses: *I'm not a good writer and I don't have time to dedicate to crafting, editing, and marketing. Plus, who am I to write a self-help book? Blah blah blah.* Even though I teach this path, I still must walk it. I killed my comfort zone and took the risk. I chose to believe I could.

So, I did, and here we are.

You, too, have the power to follow your dreams, but you must first ask yourself:

Do I want to march through life scared of the "what ifs" or do I want to live a life in which I truly come alive?

Together, you and I can put an end to making excuses, and instead, start believing your dreams are possibilities. Proverbially speaking, my teachings can't make you a supermodel, but they can give you ideas for a curve-flattering, strength-showcasing wardrobe to wear while confidently walking the runway of life.

Congratulations. Being here means you are thinking about wanting, doing, or becoming something more. That takes courage. I hope you have the audacity to take whatever next step presents itself. In the meantime, know I am holding space for you so you can step when you're ready.

Putting on your big girl pants means you're prepared to make a change for the better, no matter how negative the phrase has seemed until now. We're about to take back the meaning and take control over what's making us unhappy.

Doesn't that sound amazing?

MY STORY

*"There will be a few times in your life when all your
instincts will tell you to do something, something that defies
logic, upsets your plans, and may seem crazy to others.
When that happens, do it. Listen to your instincts and
ignore everything else. Ignore logic, ignore the odds,
ignore the complications, and just go for it."*

-Judith McNaught

It was a cold, blustery February morning and my husband
walked into the frigid weather to drive our oldest daughter
to school. His car was stuck in the driveway, the white
snow shining against the black exterior. I heard his boots
crunch the slush beneath them as he walked back toward
the house, muttering muffled phrases. *Here we go again,* I
thought, as his shouted frustrations grew closer and closer.
Just as I suspected, it wasn't long before he was inside
hurling insults at me.

This wasn't new or unusual behavior; my husband had
yelled at me for everything when he was under substantial
stress. This time, having just started a new business, he was
on edge, trying not to disappoint his family, yet taking the
pressure out on us. To compensate for his behavior, I did
what needed to be done so I didn't have to listen to him

screaming any longer: I bundled up and helped push his car out of the snowbank, sending him and my daughter on their merry way while I walked back inside to finish cleaning the kitchen. That's when I saw his wallet on the counter and knew he'd be returning. Minutes later, he stormed back in the door.

"You don't always have to take your stress out on me," I said, staring out the window over the sink. Quick to anger, he didn't speak. Instead, he picked up a bottle of cherry Nyquil and winged it against the wall, splattering crimson fluid from floor to ceiling.

"Go fuck yourself," he said as he grabbed his wallet and headed back into the frigid air.

Our relationship had become cyclical: we acted civilly, didn't speak about what was truly bothering us, and then had these outbursts proving nothing was fine. There I stood, watching the cough medicine drip down the wall and spill onto the floor, not feeling angry, defensive, or sad as I would have in the past. I'd been slowly realizing this wasn't healthy or normal for either of us, and I was emotionally detaching from him each time there was an outburst. But on this day, the day of snowmageddon (or the cough medicine apocalypse), I wasn't numb or apathetic like I once was. Instead, I felt like some magical force was sending serene vibes into my soul.

I don't have to do this anymore.
I don't have to put up with this.

I can change my life.
I am not stuck.

I had to start listening to my intuition—the truth that had been guiding me all along. Yes, my husband could be big, loud and aggressive when we argued, but that didn't mean he was completely at fault for my unhappiness. Nor was it my boundary-testing teens, protective mother, judgmental co-workers, empty bank account, or out-of-control yellow lab puppy making me miserable.

It was me.

That's the day I realized unhappiness is never anyone else's fault. I had always wanted to blame everyone else, yet I realized nothing changed when I pointed fingers at other people. *If* I was committed to making a change for the better, and *if* I wanted things to change, I had to change them myself. There was no magical do-it-for-me fairy. While the medicine began pooling on the kitchen floor, I realized I had the power to change my life.

It was time to face the truth. It was time to stop bitching and start sporting my big girl pants, not the mom jeans, yoga pants, or wine drinking, gossip-slinging country club trousers I thought I should be wearing. None of those fit or felt like me. They were all uncomfortable. What I subconsciously longed for was my own pair of custom-tailored big girl pants with a manual explaining how to wear them with power, authority, and happiness.

Fact: I wanted to get a divorce.

Fears: I might ruin my kids' lives. I probably couldn't afford a lawyer and I couldn't afford to be a single mother. My family and friends would think I was a failure. My husband would find ways to make my life a living hell.

Immediate result: Though I was unhappy in my unsalvageable marriage, I convinced myself staying married was better than what might happen if I was single.

I started digging deep, dissecting the negative things I'd told myself for a very, very long time. I knew I was unhappy in my marriage, but I stayed for a lot of reasons that seemed logical and healthy.

Once I realized how my fears held me back from going after the divorce I wanted, I saw how I was also holding myself back in other ways.

Fact: I wanted to change careers and do what I love.

Fears: If I left my job and worked for myself, I couldn't afford health insurance. The risk of failing as an entrepreneur was too big; I didn't think I could make it work.

Immediate Result: I stayed in a job that was safe but didn't make me feel alive.

Putting my big girl pants on required constant effort. I had to keep asking myself, over and over again, if the reasons I chose not to go after something I wanted were based on fear. For example, how could I possibly make being a single mom work?

Fact: I wanted to sell my house and drive a less-expensive car.

Fears: It would be too embarrassing. People in my community would judge me and deem me unworthy if I didn't keep up a certain lifestyle.

Fact: I wanted to move into a small condominium with my two teenaged daughters.

Fears: My kids would be mortified. They would be embarrassed to have friends over and it wouldn't be their home. They would hate me.

Making excuses was easy and held a valuable purpose: to protect me from doing what I so desperately wanted but was terrified to do. Damn. I believed I was safer staying where I was than having to overcome all the "what ifs." Yet, the primal whispers inside me were louder than the voices (excuses) in my head. I knew what I wanted.

Even though I had to analyze the facts and fears I was facing, that didn't automatically mean things would change. Analyzing gave me a clearer idea of what options I had moving forward, but I still had to decide when to take the first step. Hard work? Yes, but it was also rewarding and helped reshape my life.

By questioning each excuse—each paradigm I created—I evaluated the emotional cost of staying stuck.

What if all the things I am worrying about never actually happen?

What if I follow my heart and everything works out the way it's supposed to, in its own time?

As my thoughts started to change, so did my story. Within six months, I got divorced.

I didn't ruin my kids' lives and—instead—taught them about strength. Plus, my family and friends showered me with support. But the most shocking, most beautifully unexpected outcome of facing my fears and following my heart was that my ex-husband and I both became happier. We are now better friends than when we were married, and that is certainly a positive spin on an unfortunate situation (for everyone involved).

I quit my job and became a life coach, chasing down my dreams and teaching women about the very practices I was putting into play in my own life. To finance these big life changes, I sold my house and car and became debt free (which felt far greater than struggling to live beyond my means). My girls and I had the times of our lives in that condo, growing closer while making memories in our new home.

What I learned was life changing: the obstacles themselves were never the problem. The problem was the made-up stories about why I couldn't overcome the obstacles. I never even considered the fact I could do something. I simply believed I couldn't.

No wonder I was unhappy.

And yet, when I finally faced my fears and put on my big girl pants, the truth came pouring into my life as if it had been waiting for me to make a move all along.

Not one of my excuses/worst-case scenarios ever came true. Not even one.

Women (yes, that includes you) tell themselves stories, subconsciously changing their minds, words, and choices, and as a result, live in fear instead of love.

Are you doing this?

The phrase "put on your big girl pants" is often used to keep women living in fear, isn't it? To force them into "sucking it up" and doing whatever unfulfilling thing they don't want to do because "that's life" and that's what's become expected.

But what if you didn't have to accept the worst, or even mediocre? Clearly, that's the question that revolutionized my life.

I know what it's like to feel stuck, afraid and alone. I remember being too embarrassed to tell anyone the secrets I kept behind closed doors. But, I found a way out.

Just like me, you can rewrite your script, too.

That's why we're both here, after all, for you to learn the methods I teach to transform the lives of the women with whom I work. Their lives and stories will be shared throughout each chapter as further fuel and inspiration to prove you can do this.

Because you can do this.

Let me show you how.

CHAPTER 1:

BE YOU

One of the greatest tragedies in life is to lose your own sense of self and accept the version of you that is expected by everyone else.

-J.L. Toth

I spent years trying to keep up with the Joneses only to find out I didn't even like them (they were stuffy and boring). Growing up, the idyllic suburb I lived in was referred to as "The Bubble." People there didn't speak of unhappiness, discontent or misfortune. Instead, they discussed overflowing bank accounts, luxury SUVs, and historical homes. They shared stories of landscapers, tropical vacations, organic fruit, and personal trainers. Of hypoallergenic dogs, Lululemon, and All-American scholar athletes.

The Bubble left no room for error; you were expected to excel, no exceptions. And so, from an early age, I learned who I was supposed to be: smart, rich, popular, beautiful, thin, and successful.

Any other version of me was simply unacceptable.

I was already on the fast-track to success by the time I was in 7th grade; I was competitive and willing to do whatever it took to get ahead and prove myself worthy. However, my competitors were the co-eds in the elite, private all-girls school I attended, and I struggled to keep up academically, as documented by the headmaster of my school:

June 16, 1981

Dear Dr. and Mrs. Baird:

We have recently completed the year-end student review for the seventh form and Lisa's teachers have asked me to share their concerns with you.

The noticeable downward trend in Lisa's academic achievement is of concern to all. We recognize part of this is generated simply by virtue of the fact she is an adolescent with all the negative influences naturally accompanying this difficult stage of development. We also recognize adolescence alone cannot be the total answer to Lisa's problem. By every measurable indicator we have, Lisa should be doing better than she is. Her teachers tell me she is well-behaved and seemingly attentive in class. Her written homework is neatly done and shows no evidence of concern. One has only to meet Lisa and talk with her to know she is both bright and inquisitive. What then is missing? Quite frankly, we don't know.

About the only reasonable explanation we've been able to come up with is Lisa spends an inordinate amount of "thinking time" on the social intrigues of her peers. Perhaps this line of thinking occupies more time than we realize. Whatever the reason, we are all hopeful the maturity she gains over the summer will enable her to recognize the disastrous affect her present patterns have over her own academic development.

Lisa must face reality and reality requires noticeable improvement in academic effort and achievement if Lisa is to continue at this school. The intense academic atmosphere of our Upper School program mandates a firm foundation in the basics as well as a strong desire to achieve.

This has been a difficult year for Lisa. Seventh grade usually is. For some reason, eighth grade is historically less traumatic. We will all continue to hope this will be true for Lisa.

In a nutshell, I wasn't good enough. *My patterns were disastrous.* How much worse could it get?

Ashamed and not knowing what else to do, I did what any self-conscious 12-year-old girl would: I hid my insecurity. Instead of accepting myself, I hit my competition hard with insults, rumors, and drama. I bullied other people to keep the focus off what I perceived as personal inadequacies. Though negative, I got the attention I wanted. This is a dangerous defense mechanism many of us use: we compare ourselves to others and then insult whatever we see as a weakness in them.

It worked right up until my Lindsay Lohan lifestyle gifted me a suspension (yes, that's a *Mean Girls* reference). With my cover blown, I thought the humiliation of being kicked out of school for three days would suffocate me.

Surprisingly, I was relieved.

Exposing myself for who I was meant no more popularity competition, no more personal attacks. I could start over without worrying about social strata or seriously-lacking self-esteem. I learned joy came from being honest, vulnerable, and exposed. And that included loving myself, flaws and all. I didn't have to be like everyone else. I could be me. I was good enough.

Knowing Who You Are

My guess is, like most people, you have a keen ability to alter who you are in different situations, like a chameleon who changes colors. You, me, and everyone else have been blessed (or perhaps sometimes cursed) with two different selves: our **authentic selves** and our **social selves,** making all of us able to modify our personalities when we want to fit in or be accepted.

Your **authentic self** is who you are at the core. It's who you are when there is no one around to judge you or give you unwanted advice. It's the *you* stripped of expectations and who makes decisions based on what *you* want. The authentic self isn't concerned with pleasing other people; its primary role is to be the *real* you.

The **social self**, on the other hand, is who you are based on who you think you should be. Society dictates this as do the opinions of your family, friends, teachers and mentors, co-workers, and random people in the grocery store. The *social self* is the version of you who makes choices based on what's acceptable to everyone else.

The problem? It's easy to lose track of who you are when you're wrapped up in deciding who you think other people want you to be. This proves you're living your life—like many, many others do—for everyone else, not for yourself. This can result in a lifetime prescription of antidepressants.

So how do you gain awareness and apply it to your life for change?

Well, the answer involves inner-work, including asking yourself if your actions are sparked by your own beliefs and needs or by someone else's. It's complex, constant effort, but doing it means you end up happier (because it takes just as much work to decide how to act to make others happy).

Each day, you have hundreds of choices (from small ones, *chai tea or cappuccino?* to the largest, *stay married and commit or get a divorce and split?*) Yet, your choices might not always be based on being your genuine, true self. Let's take this scenario, for example:

You're invited to a party and agree to go, but as soon as you confirm, something feels off and you realize your invite acceptance was based off what you think the party-thrower wants, not what you want.

You then become frustrated with yourself: *Why did I say yes? I just want to stay home this weekend and enjoy a glass of wine and watch Netflix.*

This is when the internal struggle begins. You will feel guilty if you don't go, but you will resent yourself if you do.

This is a perfect example of being misaligned with your purpose. When your desires (stay home) and your actions (go to the party) don't match, you aren't being true to yourself. Your body (instincts) are saying, "Hell no, sister," but your thoughts are saying, "Well, maybe just for an hour or two. I don't want to hurt anyone's feelings." This a red-flag indicating you need to stop and reevaluate the situation.

You're either all in or all out, with no agenda besides being the best YOU.

REAL WOMEN'S WOES

Anna

Anna had been working in her family business for 10 years, and her father left her and her brothers in charge of the company upon retiring. Straight from college, she went into her role as a controller for the company. Graduating with a degree in finance, she worked toward becoming the company's CFO, knowing her professional life was already planned for her. So Anna marched through life doing the only thing she knew, as did the rest of her siblings, ensuring her family business stayed lucrative. She got married and had a little girl while she—day in and day out—went to work with a fake smile, carrying on with what was expected of her.

Anna disliked crunching numbers and creating long-range forecasts. Sure it came easy to her, but it bored her to tears. Her life became balance sheets and budgets—certainly not what she had in mind when she decided to start a family. She had no interest in the corporate world. All Anna wanted was to be home to watch her daughter take her first steps and say her first word. Yet, Anna loved her father and knew he worked hard to create an empire so she could live happily ever after. She didn't want to let him or her family down, but all she could think of when she was at work was being home with her baby girl.

Anna knew she wasn't cut out for a full-time career. She wanted to be a stay-at-home mother. Her husband made enough money to support her doing so, yet Anna was torn: if doing what she wanted meant letting someone else down, especially her own father, Anna wasn't so sure it was worth the heartache.

She knew who she was and what she wanted, so why was it so hard for her to make this decision? Perhaps it was because she didn't realize it was an option to do what she wanted. There was no rulebook in college saying, *Hey, guess what? You don't have to follow anyone else's path.*

I met Anna when she was still working for her dad. She shared with me several limiting beliefs she had about her life:

She was a disappointment to her father already, so she couldn't quit working for him and make it worse.

She wasn't a good mom because she was always at work.

Her husband was sick of having to keep her positive.

Yet—together—Anna and I realized these weren't things anyone said to her, they were just thoughts keeping her stuck in the life she was living (instead of living the life she wanted). What an awakening this was for Anna. When she realized she could step away from what she believed she was supposed to do, peel back the guilt enveloping her, and transform her life into what she wanted it to be, her life already felt changed without making big decisions. All she needed was permission, but not from anyone outside of herself. Anna needed her own.

Ladies, you don't have to be or do anything you don't want. You must, however, give yourself permission to follow your heart and do what you love and what fills you up. In the end, not everyone is going to agree with your choices, but when you stay true to yourself, *you* will be happy. And that is priceless.

Life is too short to live for someone else.

It's time to live for you.

HOW TO PUT YOUR BIG GIRL PANTS ON

BE YOU

Each chapter of the book holds an area for you to check in with yourself and evaluate how you relate to the concept and real-life women listed. Dig deep, truly looking at whether you mostly show up as your real or social self.

Read through the questions provided here and write your answers below (or on your own paper, if you'd prefer).

Think of a time when you were living your social self, trying to please others and fit in.

How did you act?

How did you feel?

Now, think of a time when you were totally authentic - when you said and did exactly what you wanted.

How did you act?

How did you feel?

Notice the difference?

Stop trying to build a life that merely looks good on the outside, and instead create a rewarding, fulfilling life that feels good on the inside. Happiness begins the moment you decide to be yourself, once and for all.

Figure out who you are and be that person ALL THE FREAKING TIME.

CHAPTER 2:

DECIDE HOW YOU WANT TO FEEL

We think too much and feel too little.

-Charlie Chaplin

Have you ever been asked how you want to feel, even in varying situations?

Right now, ask yourself that very question in these different scenarios:

How do you want to feel when you're:

- Spending time with the people you love most?
- Paying your bills?
- Working?
- Saying I love you?

Many people have bucket lists, to-do lists, resolutions, and goals. We fill our time desperately trying to accomplish these tasks, only to feel less than satisfied when we do.

For years, my life was booked solid. Between my daily chores, carpool schedule, career and volunteer obligations, family responsibilities, and social agenda, I was on the go 24/7. To me, this signified success. It meant my life was complete.

Except something was missing. Why wasn't hosting dinner parties, having a perfectly organized house, and climbing the corporate ladder giving me joy? It's because I thought those things would bring me happiness, and I was learning they really didn't.

I was looking for happiness in all the wrong places, chasing a feeling I thought would come by doing those things. After my divorce, I knew how much I needed to check in with myself on my actions, and I realized I reverted to my old ways, replicating what is seriously (and sadly) common for women.

I was chasing.

Happy people don't chase.

When I realized this, my world transformed again. I started creating lists and goals according to whether they would bring me the joy I desired. Not the other way around.

How did I want to feel?

I decided I wanted to feel free.

When it came down to it, I didn't like having a full, repetitive schedule. I didn't want to have to go to yoga at the same time every day. I didn't want to work from 9-5. I didn't want to say yes to every single person who wanted to have coffee or cocktails. And so, as I planned my days, I would ask myself, *does this make me feel shackled or unshackled?* I started to say no to things and commitments which no longer excited me. Free became a way of life—not just a word or concept.

I also wanted to feel (and be) authentic. I wanted to spend time around people I could be myself with. I didn't want to go to fundraisers and get all dressed up just for surface conversations. I didn't want to build my business by trying to emulate other successful coaches. I didn't want to spend my free time at the gym trying to get buff. None of that was me.

I wanted to feel like I was growing: as a person, a coach, in my personal life and in my business. I wanted to do more, see and feel more. I wanted to step outside my own comfort zone and break down my newfound fears. I wanted to say yes to scary things, pushing my own boundaries. I wanted to become more.

After I decided how I wanted to feel, I understood everything I'd been going after in my life was external. Credentials on my resume. Approval from others. Material possessions. Social status. No wonder I was apathetic; my soul wasn't being fed. I was busy, but I wasn't engaged or aligned with my life's purpose. I was stuck and unsure how to get un-stuck.

It would take bold action for me to realize I had the power to change my circumstances and get the life I wanted.

REAL WOMEN'S WOES

Lucy

Lucy came to me wanting to sign up for my most intensive coaching package. When I asked her what was going wrong in her life, she began the list: her seemingly endless string of disappointments in her dating life, her inadequate sex drive, her body fat, lack of direction and inability to get organized, too. Her friends were judgmental and she felt like a hot mess. She was in her mid-thirties and was nowhere near where she thought she'd be. Her list went on and on.

When I asked her the simple, yet powerful, question, "how do you want to feel at the end of the day?" she leaned back in her chair and folded her arms like a pretzel.

"I want to feel like somebody wants me," she said.

I asked the question again, emphasizing the words *you* and *feel* because her answer was still about someone else and how they felt. Frustrated, she broke into tears.

"I've never thought about it. My whole life, I have tried to please everyone else. I don't know how I want to feel."

After some thought, Lucy told me she wanted to feel energized. She wanted to stop complaining and start loving the parts of her life going well (and improve the negative parts). She no longer wanted to play the victim role. Her work schedule left her exhausted, the weight kept her from feeling beautiful, and she didn't want to live like this anymore.

Instead, she wanted to feel passion, freedom, and inspiration. When she committed to finally making choices based on these feelings, not what worked best for everyone else, Lucy's whole world began to expand.

Elizabeth

Elizabeth, one of my college-bound clients, was struggling to see eye-to-eye with her parents. She was highly stressed and was applying to every school she could. When I asked her where she wanted to go, she exclaimed, "My mom wants me to go to The Ohio State University for undergrad and then on to medical school."

Her glossed-over eyes, drooping head, and slumped shoulders told me how she felt about what her mom wanted.

"How does this make *you* feel when you think about this path?" I asked.

"I don't want to go to a big school. I want to go to a small school out of state but my mom would kill me. She wants me to be a doctor because my dad is a doctor."

She paused, looked directly at me and instantly appeared to be engulfed by purpose.

"I want to go into retail merchandising. I love fashion." She drew out the "a" in fashion like she was hanging from it.

Elizabeth decided she wanted to feel boundless. She realized she could either follow the path her parents wanted for her or she could follow her own path—the one *she* desired. She understood she was not an extension of her mother and father; she was her own individual who needed to nourish her desires, even though they were scary to confront.

Once she started feeling and acting boundless, Elizabeth started being boundless. She followed her heart and ended up going to a small, community art school— close to home like her parents wanted—but in a field she dreamed about.

What do these two women—at very different stages in life—have in common?

Lucy and Elizabeth worried more about pleasing everyone else than making themselves truly, deeply happy. They were acting from their social selves, not their authentic selves. Neither stopped to determine what might be best for them, and they needed to cut through the layers of social conditioning, shed the expectations of others, and follow their individual, internal maps. They needed to discover how they wanted to feel in their lives and then make their choices based on that.

So let me ask you:

Are you doing the same thing?

Your intuition is your greatest guide. Listen to it carefully; it will nudge you in the direction of your dreams just like it did for Lucy and Elizabeth.

Are your choices in alignment with your authentic self? They are if they're based on who you are and what feels right to you. When your choices feel right and sync up with your dreams, magical things happen. You enter a space where you're ready to start thinking about what you want—what you really, really want—in life.

HOW TO PUT YOUR BIG GIRL PANTS ON

DECIDE HOW YOU WANT TO FEEL

How would you like to feel every day? There's no right or wrong way to answer this. Just get the words out of your head and onto this sheet of paper (or another one).

Write your word(s) here:

Now, find the most appealing word you wrote down. You can have them all, yes, but we need to start getting you acquainted with this practice with a more manageable step.

For the next few days, try to base your choices, words, and actions on that feeling. Then try it for a week. Then a month.

Keep going.

You will eventually start living every facet of your life based on the feelings you desire.

Life will feel more purposeful and plentiful.

CHAPTER 3:

DREAM BIGGER

*The future belongs to those who believe in the beauty of
their dreams.*

-Eleanor Roosevelt

We all have dreams.

Whether your dream is traveling the world, dropping
weight, organizing your desk, or running for public office,
we all desire something.

For most of us, our dreams surface instinctively when
we are young and able to make choices based on our
desires, not fears. When my youngest daughter was seven,
she wanted to be a teacher. She was only in 2nd grade, but
every time I bought her new pencils and notebooks she
asked if we could play school. I played the student, an
adult crunched in her tiny, toddler chair and she was the
teacher, of course.

Her confidence struck me. She never asked if she was
good enough or smart enough to be a teacher, nor did she
ask me if she would be able to control the unruly students

or deal with nasty coworkers. She just liked pretending to be a teacher: taking attendance, showing me how to do math problems, and assigning me art projects.

My daughter rocked her imaginary career.

As a former college-level English teacher, I understood working in education was no day at the beach. I knew all about administrative BS and compulsory testing and core curriculum issues - but I didn't tell her. She was seven. Instead, I loved watching her bask in the confidence of knowing she was a kick-ass instructor.

Why then, was I afraid when she grew up and entered the real world, she would lose her poise, sense of adventure, and wonder? Because I've witnessed it repeatedly, in myself first and then in my clients. People constantly doubt themselves and question whether they are doing something the right way, because they fall back into the social-self trap, basing their choices on what they see everyone else doing.

It's easy to see this when we talk about other people, right? You're probably reading and nodding your head in agreement with me. But what if I turn the questions directly toward you?

Do you believe forging your own path means you will never be successful? Is your definition of success determined by what everyone else thinks?

How often do you do what's most popular or pleasing instead of what's best for you?

Now, don't beat yourself up.

In modern society, fantasizing about an ideal life is a ridiculed, ridiculous activity. People often scold themselves when they set lofty, hopeful and whimsical goals, and they certainly don't invest in the future by taking the necessary action to make their dreams happen. Instead, people do what appears to be normal.

It's a lousy way to live.

I wish when I was younger I had learned how to daydream my ideal day while ultimately designing my life. Instead, after college, I decided to find a corporate job, pinning myself behind a desk from 9-5 everyday.

I applied for a copywriting position at the local newspaper and, as luck would have it, got the job. Finally, I was going to be someone important, with a career I could rock in the Banana Republic suits I bought.

That only lasted about six months.

Had I known then what I know now, I could have looked myself in the mirror and said, *Honey, you're kidding yourself.* I wasn't meant to be sitting at a desk all day in a business suit. I was destined to do, see and explore more, but my bank account and my brain told me I had to stay put. After all, I needed to follow this path for the rest of my life because I had a Bachelor of Arts degree and majored in English. This is what people with these credentials do.

But I couldn't sit still.

I knew there was something bigger and better for me— something more. My desire for more was stronger than my resistance, and a month after realizing I was not meant to take the typical road, I packed up my belongings and moved across the country to Montana where I got a job as a travel agent.

I didn't follow the unspoken rules, and somehow—eventually—became far more successful than I ever would have if I continued to climb the corporate ladder. My success was based on a full heart and a sense of adventure, not on what would have looked good on my curriculum vitae.

But perhaps you don't know what you want—and that's okay, too—because sometimes not knowing leads to knowing. It's a useful, important piece of the journey. Did I know I would end up as a life coach when I was hauling ass as a copywriter? Nope. Did I know I'd leave my husband after 18 years of marriage? Not until the Nyquil flew. I just had to learn to roll with the punches, make tough, risky choices, and follow my intuition along the way.

This is where dreaming bigger comes in. You have to follow your bliss or an interest, or maybe even discontentment sometimes, until your purpose is found. To do this, know your dreams serve a purpose, even if you can't see the connection in the moment. Dreaming bigger means you still take one step after another in the direction of your growth.

After time has passed and you can look back, you will see the patterns, the wisdom, the understanding, and the purpose of it all.

REAL WOMEN'S WOES

Catherine

Catherine constantly worried she wasn't a good mother. Growing up, her mom was there for her 24/7. Her mother fixed all her meals, drove her to all her activities and attended every sporting event. She also put on the most amazing birthday parties. Catherine thought her mom was superwoman.

When Catherine had children of her own, she believed she had to follow in her mother's footsteps. The only problem was, she didn't enjoy doing the things her mom, or her friends who were stay-at-home mothers, did. She despised playing with Barbie dolls and Playdoh. She didn't like volunteering in the classroom, going to music lessons or even sitting in on story time at the library. Catherine felt overwhelming guilt for wanting to do less than what her mom had done for her, and she kept this secret to herself for years, worrying her friends, and especially her mother, would judge her.

When I met Catherine she immediately confessed her feelings, admitting she was embarrassed she didn't have the motherly instincts she thought she should have. When I asked her what she wanted to do, she started to glow.

"I want to go back to work. Someday I want to start my own advertising agency," she said. Catherine knew exactly what she wanted, yet the next words out of her mouth sucked all the energy and enthusiasm out of our conversation.

"I can't," she muttered slowly, "because I need to stay home to raise my children. I should prioritize being a mother."

She became deflated.

This unrelenting feeling of guilt can plague every one of us. You know what it's like to want one thing but believe you have to do something else, don't you? This is when the social self starts overpowering the authentic self and causes you to spend half your life doing what you think must be done—not what you want.

If I had a dollar for every person I talked to who felt this way, I'd be a wealthy woman.

Like so many others, Catherine talked herself into believing working outside the home was not an option, so she went to the park and rode on the merry-go-round for hours on end, all the while spinning in physical and emotional circles. She wanted to jump off but didn't know how.

After questioning all her fears and realizing each of them were simply excuses for keeping her from going back to work, Catherine scheduled a meeting with her old boss to talk about options. After they spoke, she walked out empowered, feeling able to conquer life: the exact feelings she identified wanting in our first consultation together. As I suspected, Catherine's boss welcomed her back with open arms, suggesting she slowly work her way back into the agency by creating her own work hours and doing what felt right to her. I will never forget her call to me when she heard this news. All I could hear was pure joy. Had Catherine stayed stuck in her story, she would have kept running on the hamster wheel for years and years, never truly finding peace or balance within herself or with her family she loved so dearly.

What a sad story that would have been for this rock star woman.

If you are struggling with something in your life and have no clue as to why, I totally get it. This is something we all deal with, even those of us who do this work for a living.

Whether you know what you want or not, deep inside you there is a knowing. You might be so busy seeking happiness, however, you overlook amazing opportunities. Don't block your own success and stay stuck.

Instead, use each day to learn more, constantly designing the life meant for you—only you—and remembering the design won't look the same as your best friends' or parents'. Your design will be unique to you.

Which leads to the biggest revelation yet:

You get to decide on every single detail of your life. You design everything!

Since you get to choose how your next step will manifest in your life (who you hang out with, what you spend time on, how you pursue your passions), you will need to start thinking about it in a concrete way.

Imagine yourself sitting at a fashion designer's desk: the surface area covered in pages of fresh, white paper. With a pencil in hand, you're ready to sketch out how each day will go, and you dream up and draw out the ideal 24 hours from a peace-filled morning to restful evening.

Who decides? YOU.

It might seem scary, but the key is to keep designing regardless of your fear. You can't stop and deny your dreams. Just acknowledge your fear and let it be, turning away from the negative and taking steps toward anything that makes you feel amazing.

HOW TO PUT YOUR BIG GIRL PANTS ON

DREAM BIGGER

A vision board is a great tool to help you:

- Identify your goals and dreams
- Reinforce your daily affirmations
- Keep your attention on your intentions.

Creating a vision board helps set the intention to bring your desires to life. It's a visual representation of your goals and a way to see them before they truly exist in your world.

Four Steps to Creating a Powerful Vision Board

First, you will need:

Cardboard or poster board, markers, scissors, glue, and any art supplies you want to use.

1. Envision how you want your life to look one year from today. For example, what are some things you want to have? How would you like

to feel? Where would you like to go? What would you like to do? Etc.

2. Collect magazines and newspapers containing words, photographs, or inspirational quotes representing whatever you visualized in step one.

3. Cut out and paste these items on your board.

4. Place your creation somewhere where you can look at it every day: your office, the bathroom, or kitchen, for example.

Tech-Savvy option: Create a vision board on Pinterest and take a screen shot to use as your phone's background.

Remember: You have the power to make your visions and dreams a reality. Whatever they may be, keep in mind who you are and how you want to feel when these desires become reality.

CHAPTER 4:

FACE UNCOMFORTABLE FITS

Too often we enjoy the comfort of opinion without the discomfort of thought.

-John F. Kennedy

Deciding to put myself out into the world as a life coach was one of the scariest things I have ever done.

Do people even know what a life coach is?

Am I good enough to help other people?

Do I need to be more experienced before I promote myself?

What if, because of some of the choices I have made in my life, people don't think I'm worthy of being a coach?

What if I never get any clients?

The list went on and on, yet if I was going to build a career around helping other people do that which scared the crap out of them, I had to take the same risks myself. I needed to feel the fear and then move forward anyway.

The morning I finally decided to publish my professional life coach page on Facebook, I literally felt like I was going to be sick. Putting myself and my business out there for the world to see felt like standing in the middle of a freeway, waiting to get run over by people's judgments. Yes, becoming visible in my business felt like I was intentionally making myself a target for the naysayers.

Yet, I promoted it anyway.

The universe brought me to be that moment, and who the hell was I to fight with destiny? I knew no matter how much planning I did before putting my business out there, I'd always feel scared and—maybe—unprepared. Doing something new, no matter how qualified we are, is still frightening.

That morning, I told my boyfriend I was going to be publishing my new business page and was scared to death. He had been my biggest fan, so I wanted him to know I was going to be curled up in the fetal position when he got home if no one had "liked" my page. Intermittently throughout the day, I would check my computer to see if there was any action on my post. By about 11:00 am, I had received almost 200 likes. Yet, I noticed that my boyfriend still hadn't liked it. By 1:00 pm, he still hadn't. Same with 2:00 pm and 3:00 pm. I was steaming. The one person who knew my greatest fear wasn't supporting me.

Instead of being thrilled that so many people had already validated and encouraged my endeavor thus far, these are how my thoughts went:

11:00 am   I can't believe he didn't like my page.
11:30 am   He must not really love me.
11: 32 am   He doesn't think I'm good enough to coach.
11:59 am   Is he embarrassed by me?
12:45 pm   If he can't support my Facebook post, how is he going to support me throughout our lives?
1:37 pm   He is going to be a terrible step-dad to my kids.
1:55 pm   He doesn't love me.
2:40 pm   He doesn't respect me.
2:41 pm   He doesn't care about my feelings.
3:50 pm   I don't like him anymore.
4:39 pm   I have made a grave mistake dating this person.
5:00 pm   He never really loved me in the first place.
6:00 pm   I'm breaking up with him when he gets home tonight.

At 7: 00 pm, he walked through the door, and gave me a huge hug and kiss just like every other night. Still fuming from the day's thoughts, I shimmied out of his embrace and walked into the other room, huffing like a protesting child.

Confused, he asked what was wrong and I gave him my standard answer when I am pissed.

"Nothing. "

Even though I was mad, I knew this behavior was ridiculous. I questioned if it had anything to do with my boyfriend or everything to do with my own insecurities. As I sat alone in the other room pouting, I went through each of the thoughts I had all day, seeing each one for what it was: a judgment of myself. I decided to find the truth hidden within my story and to get out of my own head.

I took a breath and marched my butt back to my man and told him I was sorry. He didn't understand what I was apologizing for, but again, this was more about me than him. I let my sad girl story of rejection and failure go, and I let the love back in.

Mindsets, or the way people are naturally predisposed to think, are powerful. They can control, persuade, and hold us back from doing things in life. Mindsets are dangerous whenever we feel worried, scared, or uncertain, but only if we remain unaware and make decisions based on limiting beliefs we carry. Anytime we think about stepping outside of our comfort zone, our bodies naturally try to fight off whatever is deemed a risk.

Let's say you want to quit your job. The first thing that happens is your critter brain (the worry center) says, *Hell no, there is no way I can do that.* It signals fear and unpredictability, causing a physical reaction to a mental problem. Next, your limbic system (the part of the brain associated with motivation, emotion, learning, and memory) comes up with a multitude of excuses to support your initial reaction. *I will never find another job. I can't afford to quit.* Finally, the cortex (active in justifying choices and behaviors) comes up with reasons to back out. *I'm not* that *miserable. Things will get better if I stay here.* Thus, without even realizing it, you successfully talk yourself out of what you want before giving yourself time to support your desires.

There is good news, however: You have the power to stop this madness.

When thoughts kick into high gear, you can change the way you think and feel about any situation. Cool, right? Inner dialogue is meant to keep you safe because rejecting your ideas and dreams before you act helps you avoid failure and rejection from others. But the truth is, many people avoid following their instincts because they are too afraid. Why? The list of reasons is endless, but here are a few things that keep women from putting on their big girl pants:

- **Fear of embarrassment:** What if I speak to an audience and my message doesn't resonate with people?

- **Fear of guilt:** Will making a different choice upset my mom?

- **Fear of failure:** What if I start my own business and don't make any money?

- **Fear of the unknown:** Will I ever be happy again if I leave my husband?

- **Fear of rejection:** What if my co-workers don't support me when I share my thoughts at our next meeting?

- **Fear of judgment:** What will our neighbors think when we sell the house?

- **Fear of abandonment:** What if I tell my best friend how I feel and she doesn't want to hang out anymore?

It doesn't matter if you are five and are worried about monsters under your bed or if you are fifty and worried about becoming a bag lady, fears mess with your head, feed off your uncertainty, and grow until stopped.

How then, do you end this self-sabotage? By getting comfortable feeling discomfort. Being uncomfortable in a situation means your body is trying to tell you something is off. When you feel this, it doesn't automatically mean you need to turn and move in the opposite direction. Instead, follow this process:

Step One: Notice your thoughts.

My guess is you go about your day—all day—without acknowledging you have hundreds and thousands of thoughts. But when you start to listen to your inner voice, you can meet it with understanding and compassion.

Think of your internal dialogue as waves in the ocean. They ebb and flow, some negative and others positive. The secret isn't in trying to stop the waves but to start riding them. Notice when they support you and when they don't.

Step Two: Question your thoughts.

Ask yourself if what you are thinking and believing is true. Every time you have a thought that wreaks havoc with your soul, ask this simple question:

Is it true?

Determining whether or not your thoughts or beliefs are true—or if they are just stories you tell yourself—will help eliminate 99.9% of the drama in your life.

Knowing the difference between *real pain* and *imagined pain* is a game changer.

Real pain is pain we feel physically or emotionally. For example, getting hit by a car or losing a parent can cause real pain.

Imagined pain, on the other hand, is pain that comes from our thoughts or interpretations from an event. For example, was it true that my boyfriend wasn't happy for me when I started my business? No, it was a story I told myself. Was it true that Catherine—who wanted to go back to work—was a bad mother because she didn't want to stay at home? No, but she believed that narrative until she asked this question.

Let's say you are playing tennis with a co-worker. Her serve rivals one of the Williams sisters and her ball hits you directly in the forehead. You get a concussion. That is real pain. But to say that your opponent intentionally hurt you because she secretly wants your job would be perceived, emotion-driven (imagined) pain.

See the difference?

Now, consider that your grandmother passed away. Her death would cause real pain, loss and grief. In this case, it's okay to be emotional and grieve. However, if you're telling yourself stories about how you should be handling her death, or if you are feeling guilty about how much time you spent with her, you need to ask yourself the question above. More than likely, you are creating your own, imagined pain.

It is important to understand the cause of your pain. If it's real pain, it will heal over time and you can help the process along by taking care of yourself, but if you determine the pain to be imagined, questioning the negative belief you carry will be what helps you heal and prevents you from carrying an insecurity forward.

Once you learn to decipher between the truth and your story, your life will begin to change. I promise. Reality is a much better place to live.

When your mind is working with you rather than against you, your options moving forward will expand. In time and with practice, you will see a supportive, growth-inducing way through life's changes. You'll figure out these changes won't hurt you, but ignoring them—which is a common societal misstep—does. Instead of hiding from a new existence, allow yourself to align your thoughts with the potential positive outcomes.

Let your story go and let a new perception in.

REAL WOMEN'S WOES

Alison

Alison told herself her husband didn't love her anymore. She went to work feeling sad each day because she felt he was emotionally unavailable and no longer interested in her. Eventually, she began to accept this life and believed an unfulfilling marriage was all she could have, so Alison started to emotionally detach from her husband, too.

One summer at her class reunion, she ran into an old boyfriend who was nurturing and attentive—two things she craved in her marriage for years, though she never told her husband what she missed in their relationship. Over the next few months, she and her old flame became closer and more intimate. Life began to feel exciting again, and she considered breaking things off with her husband and moving on.

In all of our sessions together, I challenged Alison on her belief that her husband didn't love her anymore. Alison was unsure if he did, but she had no concrete proof that he didn't.

This realization on her part forced Alison to find the answers, so she asked her husband how he felt about their relationship. Alison's husband was relieved to be invited into a conversation about their feelings. He too was feeling disconnected and unhappy, and he could tell Alison was pulling away from him.

"I miss and love you," he said. "I want my wife—and our life—back."

Alison realized her husband *did* love her, even though they both stopped working on their marriage. The flame died out as life got busier and harder, and she was just as responsible for the fizzle as anyone. Her story of being unloved became so loud, she forgot to explore her options within her marriage. Once she realized her story was based on feelings instead of facts, Alison was able to fully recommit herself to her husband and their relationship.

What would have happened to their relationship if this conversation never happened?

The stories we tell ourselves can be dangerous and convincing, especially when they make us feel small or desperate for a new reality we don't even really want. Fear can convince us to lie to ourselves, even if we think something is for our own good. Lies masquerade as a protection mechanism and make us feel foolish when we question them. Alison's fear of rejection caused her to think her husband didn't love her, and she believed her fear and the story that went along with it.

HOW TO PUT YOUR BIG GIRL PANTS ON

FACE YOUR FEARS

Think about the fears you currently cater to in your life. Is any of your pain an emotional response? How much of it is stemming from a factual truth? If you fear losing your job or a spouse or all of your money, is your concern rooted in an unstable reality where these negative situations could really happen, or are you bracing for a worst-case scenario?

List three goals or dreams.

Next, for each list item above, write down one excuse you make for not going after them.

Now, ask yourself if any of your excuses are *actually* true.

CHAPTER 5:

IT'S OKAY TO CHANGE

Never too old, never too bad, never too late to start from scratch again.

-Bikram Choudhury

My freshman year of college, I dated a boy I couldn't see often. We met over the summer and I fell madly in love with him. Needless to say, I was devastated when I had to leave for school in Chicago that fall, but had faith our love could withstand the distance.

Over time, however, our nightly phone calls consistently became shorter and more strained. I was busy meeting people and trying to adjust to my new surroundings, and he, a junior, was juggling work, classes, and fraternity life at his school in Ohio. It wasn't that we didn't want to talk to each other as much, but our schedules made it hard. As the first semester progressed, I didn't necessarily think anything was wrong (besides our busy schedules), but I knew we were overdue for some in-person time. He had grown somewhat distant, but I assumed he was frustrated by the difficulty of a long-distance relationship. I had grown frustrated too, but more so by my expanding waistline than anything else. (I was well on my way to packing on the freshman 15.)

In our time apart, I often daydreamed about seeing him and knew we would be back on track in no time, having incredible moments like we used to.

If only we were in the same zip code.

I knew there was one way to solve this problem, so I planned a road trip to visit him the following weekend.

Besides the physical discomfort of my clothes feeling restrictive, the drive to Ohio was magical, every mile bringing me closer and closer to my true love and our time together. I listened to sappy songs and fantasized about seeing him, until, finally, I arrived at his place.

Dropping my bag outside of the car, I rushed to the front steps of his apartment and rang the doorbell.

He was wearing the jeans I loved paired with a new, more studious plaid shirt. His hair was longer, framing his face and contrasting the clean cut of his outfit. I smiled as I noticed the subtle changes in his appearance. *He looked different, too*, I thought, secretly wondering if he noticed the transformations (extra pounds) on me.

"Hey, Lis. Good to see you," he said, brushing past me toward my car. "Where's your stuff?"

Stunned, I pointed toward the side of my car. His reaction, lacking any ounce of love or romance, confirmed something was wrong.

"It's so good to see you, too," I said, following him to my car as he grabbed my bags.

I tried to drape myself around him, but he blocked my embrace by gently pushing me away. He seemed to look me up and down, taking in all of my body like it was new.

Our exchange was nothing like what I wanted or expected: no romantic kiss or long hug or sexy gaze, but I'd just gotten there and wasn't ready to admit defeat yet. *Maybe he was just tired or hungry, or maybe he was acting funny because we hadn't seen each other in so long.* But fear and doubt were creeping in as quickly as the excuses I made for him. *Maybe he thinks I'm gross.* Unsure which of those thoughts might be true, I decided to try my hardest to make the weekend memorable.

"What do you want to do tonight?" I asked.

"How 'bout we stop by Taco Bell?" he replied.

"Great," I said, silently starting to believe my weight was the cause of his distance. I was starving, but his once over just minutes before made me feel ashamed of my body.

I reached for his hand, longing to touch him, but he took it like I was his sister and we were at church reciting *Our Father.* He wasn't completely rude, but he was certainly detached and unenthusiastic.

We rode in silence on the way to Taco Bell. I recounted every minute since I'd made it to Ohio, wondering what I did wrong, and trying hard to hide my disappointment. Yet, as soon as we went inside to order, I knew the unhappiness

I felt wasn't made up or exaggerated. He was *definitely* behaving differently.

"Welcome to Taco Bell. What can I get you guys?" The teenager behind the counter stared and waited for a response.

"A cheesy double beef burrito for me," my boyfriend said before turning to meet my gaze. "And a water for her."

Dammit. I thought. *I'm famished.* But I didn't say anything to him. He was clearly not thrilled about my appearance, and I didn't want to make matters worse.

In that moment, my brain started racing and I felt inadequate:

You aren't good enough for him anymore.

He'd love you if you weren't fat.

You are the reason tonight isn't going as planned.

I sipped my water and sulked while my stomach growled. *What happened to the boyfriend I loved? Why did I have to gain so much weight?* There wasn't much conversation at Taco Bell. I felt overlooked, unappreciated, and ashamed, but there was no way in hell I was going to tell him that.

"I'm going to stop and get some beer," he announced, glancing at the minimart across the street.

"Oh, okay. I'll go in with you," I said, staring out the window of Taco Bell and hoping he'd hurry up and eat so our awkwardness could be less public.

"If you want."

As if what I want matters to you, I thought.

We drove across the street and I hopped out of the car, determined to get a snack to silence my rumbling stomach. Embarrassed, I didn't want him to know I was hungry, so I casually walked through the aisles, scanning the store for a place hidden from the cashier. I already resigned myself to stealing food so I could hide my hunger from my jerk of a boyfriend.

I pumped myself up for whatever snacks awaited me. I wouldn't be picky; any sweet or salty treat would do.

While my guy was buying beer, I bent down and grabbed a Skor bar, slipped it in my coat pocket, and stood up, walking straight out of the store toward the car.

My boyfriend remained silent the rest of the trip back to his place. Hungry, I told him I wanted to shower after my long ride, so I headed to the bathroom, a safe place to devour my goods.

After starting the water, I got undressed and peeled the wrapper off the Skor bar, trying to decide where I should hide my trash. Leaving it next to my clothes, I hopped into the shower to make sure he didn't grow suspicious of me. Plus, I felt so gross after the unexpected turn of events, I wanted to wash off the day.

Standing in the hot, comforting water, I felt okay; for a moment I was alone and none of the other crap happening mattered. Refocusing on my hunger, I started to eat the candy.

The heat of the shower melted the chocolate, and it was dripping through my tight grip.

"What the hell are you doing?!" I heard as someone threw back the shower curtain.

There he was, standing in the bathroom with the wrapper in hand, my guy disgustedly looking at my fat ass and the chocolate dripping down my fingers and lips.

"Whaaa?" was all I could say with a mouth full of chocolate.

He turned, revolted, and walked back out of the bathroom. Meanwhile, I stood naked, candy bar in hand, as the steaming water ran over my body.

The gig was up. He knew what I was doing, so I reached forward and pushed the curtain closed as far as I could before shrugging. I wasn't sure what awaited me back in his room, but I knew I had at least four more bites of chocolate left to enjoy before I'd find out.

When I walked into his bedroom, he was waiting for me. He looked detached and annoyed. I knew it meant we were about to break up.

Is he going to dump me because I gained a few extra pounds?

Or is it because he just busted me eating in the shower?

In a blur of my own thoughts, I didn't listen as he spoke. I hit what I could only describe as rock bottom when he suggested we "cool things off." I was devastated, unable to see how my weight warranted that type of judgment and punishment.

I cried and cried and cried all the way back to Chicago. Not only was I losing a boyfriend and feeling rejected, but I was feeling like a fat cow.

I was an absolute mess.

Looking back on college-me, I want to smack her ample ass and say, *wake up*! However, I cannot go back in time and give myself the kick in the booty I so clearly needed. Instead, I have to accept that even after I was humiliated in that bathroom, I still needed to deal with my self-loathing before I did the hard work required to love myself completely.

Yes, our relationship was shallow. I didn't understand that at the time, but why didn't I at least see how much I was shrinking in his presence? I wish I could have said something like, *Dude, did you seriously just order me a water for dinner?*

Why didn't I call him out on it? I suppose preserving my image was more important than respecting myself and what I wanted. I knew I never wanted to be treated that way again, but I wasn't sure how to avoid it.

After a period of mourning, I realized our relationship was incredibly unhealthy. I gave myself permission to change my pants, switch directions, and never again to go out with guys who didn't appreciate me. I decided I didn't want to hang out with people who expected me to be a certain way. No more being a submissive woman for me, which basically meant I wouldn't have to hide in the bathroom when I wanted to eat a candy bar. Win.

Real Women's Woes

Leslie

Leslie sat at her dining room table with 350 wedding invitations in front of her; she had taken a calligraphy-writing workshop and was ready to start addressing them one by one. The venue, band, and menu for her special day were thoughtfully chosen, and deposits paid. She agreed on the flower arrangements, cake flavors, and professional photographer her mother helped her pick out. Her dress was ready for its final hem and her bag was packed for her wedding night. Everything was ready to go.

Everything, except Leslie.

Leslie had a deep, dark secret she never intended to tell anyone, and it tugged at her heart with every envelope she meticulously addressed: she was not in love with her fiancé.

They started dating in high school and being with him was comfortable, but she didn't feel the spark she wished she had going into the biggest day of her life. She knew in her heart she couldn't get married in six weeks, but the shame, embarrassment, and guilt of calling off her wedding were just too much for her to handle. She had to go forward with her plans. There was no other option.

She felt stuck and began mentally preparing to live an exceptionally uninspiring life.

The invitations were all addressed, stamped and ready to be mailed. They looked like a professional had inscribed them and she was proud of herself. *I can do this*, Leslie continually repeated to herself. *This is the life I am supposed to live.*

As she drove them to the post office, the voice inside her head became progressively louder. She could feel the pounding of her heart - the calling to follow her soul's deepest desire. Yet, Leslie found herself stuck at a crossroad. *Should she turn left and go back home or should she go straight ahead and mail the invitations?* Her heart knew the answer, but her head fought to keep her on the familiar, safe path.

In her heart, Leslie knew the way.

She knew marrying her fiancé was unfair to both of them, so she turned away from that marriage toward a new journey, the one she knew was hers to be had all along.

It's not uncommon for people to sit at the same exact stop sign, talking themselves into something they intuitively know is wrong. Like Leslie and others, you might not know which way to turn (or maybe you do, but fear making a move). Believe your truths unashamedly— because the truth always knows the way.

You are who you are. Nothing more, nothing less.

Your sudden revelations may not be as impactful as breaking off an engagement, but the cumulative effect of these choices can lead to monumental moments requiring intense decision-making. If you want to avoid the major drama and heartbreak, you need to follow your heart as you make small decisions. Otherwise, they will add up.

Trust and be true to your desires each step along the way.

HOW TO PUT YOUR BIG GIRL PANTS ON

IT'S OKAY TO CHANGE YOUR PANTS

Just by knowing what we don't want, we can be open to what we do—or will—want with time and personal growth.

What big things in your life would you want to change? For example, your health? Your career? Your relationships?

What small things need to be done differently?

If my life had absolutely no limits, what would I choose to have?

What would I choose to do?

What do I *not* like to do?

CHAPTER 6:

DON'T COMPARE PANTS

"If you are willing to look at another person's behavior toward you as a reflection of the state of their relationship with themselves rather than a statement about your value as a person, then you will, over a period of time cease to react at all."

-Yogi Bhajan

Sometimes you see other women walking down the street in pants that make their bodies look phenomenal, and it's easy to—in those moments—want what they have. It's easy to think that by getting the pants *she's* wearing you will feel better, stronger or sexier, but it's time to prove this type of logic is absolutely wrong.

Comparison is a beast of an issue, one keeping you from feeling good about yourself no matter what your intentions are.

Think of it this way:

We both have and wear cute pants. However, our bodies are shaped differently. Just because your pants look good on you, doesn't mean they'll look good on me (and vice versa). That doesn't mean there is something wrong with either of us, it just means we are different people who wear clothing in different ways (and we should wear what works for our own body type).

It's time to stop comparing.

Get out of other people's pants already, okay?

One of the best ways to help yourself grow is to focus on your own proverbial pants.

Think how much time a day you spend noticing what other people are doing or should be doing.

She shouldn't be spending so much time going out with her friends when she doesn't even have time to pick the weeds out of her front yard.

She's not all that great at her job. I don't think she deserved that promotion.

Does she realize she's too old to wear shorts that short?

I wonder if she notices her husband spends more time looking at other women than he does her.

You will never find peace and harmony in your own life when all your energy is being spent on what's wrong with everyone else. Work to start caring less about what others are doing and more about what you're doing.

Let me ask you this: What do any of these judgments have to do with you?

Look in the mirror.

For years, it would drive me nuts when my mom would try to control me. I spent hours on end complaining about it to anyone who would listen. The thing is, I learned what drove me nuts about my mother was the exact thing I didn't like about myself: *I* was controlling. My controlling nature complicated my relationships, made me lose sleep and robbed me of happiness. Yet, displacing this on my mom took away any ownership I had about my own faults. Once I realized this simple thing, *what I see in others reflects what I see in myself,* I could stop complaining and start fixing myself.

The same goes for you.

Do you judge others? Take a long, hard look in the mirror because we notice in other people what we know to be true in ourselves. Our beliefs about someone else are our own insecurities or blunders flaring up.

To reiterate:

The most annoying, most rage-inducing tendencies in others are subconsciously showing you your own insecurities.

The good news? Once you start to recognize insecurities for what they are, those beliefs lose their power over you.

Decide what you want to see in the mirror.

You have power and control over your circumstances. Don't ever forget that or you'll become a person who allows her life stories to become debilitating. When you believe you've lost control and surrender responsibility for addressing a problem you face, past stories become current realities and excuses for unhappiness, unworthiness, and suffering. In this place, you become a victim, and victims feel safe with their stories because clinging to them is so much easier than having to write new ones.

Perhaps your mother favored your sister while growing up and you always felt unimportant or unloved.

Or your stepmom took all the family money when your dad passed away.

Maybe you got pregnant and had to change your future plans.

Yes, you've likely been hurt, felt sorry for yourself, or wallowed in your own misery, but—more importantly—

you can also change how you feel in any situation and write a different ending.

I recently had lunch with a friend who reverts to her story every time I talk to her. On this occasion, the dressing on Julie's Tuna Nicoise salad was too heavy, so she complained to the waiter and had him remake it. I knew what was coming: her woe-is-me story.

It never fails.

Somehow, Julie segued her salad debacle right into her home foreclosure, which, by the way, happened many, many years ago. In two sentences, she went from dressing to drama as she began to recount negative anecdotes of her struggle to pay her bills when she was first married.

Why? Because the wounds from Julie's past are still there, ready to come to the surface whenever the little things in life don't go her way. The salad dressing was the catalyst for the day's negativity, giving her permission to open the floodgates to the real, unresolved issue.

When you look at yourself in the mirror, you must be conscious of the reality you describe to yourself. What you see and what is there may not always match. If you aren't careful, you can convince yourself your situation is worse than it really is.

Julie is not alone. Her cocoon is her story, and to break out of it would be far too scary. What might she discover? Happiness? Maybe. But to her, and many other people, the unknown is riskier than replaying her unhappiness on a constant loop. Her story remains her life and that by which all things, big and small, are defined. Her negativity breeds negativity. Day in and day out. She is what happened to her all those many years ago.

Perhaps you have a story. Is it time for you to compose a different ending? No matter where you are along the journey, your story isn't over yet. What are you going to do to change the ending (yes, even if you're in the middle of something big)?

REAL WOMEN'S WOES

Holly and Amanda

Holly and Amanda were colleagues who loved working together but both hated their teaching jobs. They were burnt out even though they still enjoyed aspects of working with kids and working together.

One day, Amanda made the decision she couldn't continue working in a job she disliked. She talked to the people on her team and shared how her discontentment was outweighing the joy she used to feel working with students. Meanwhile, Holly alternated between cheering for Amanda and crying for herself. She wanted to leave, too, but she wasn't ready. Amanda knew how conflicted her friend felt and struggled to find the balance between preparing to move on and encouraging her friend to also take the leap.

Amanda wanted to help. The truth is, she wanted Holly to do exactly what she had done: leave her job and pursue her life's passion. However, Holly wasn't ready to take the action steps needed to shift away from a secure job as a teacher to something risky like consulting work. Amanda grew more and more frustrated with Holly's inability to act, and as a result, their relationship became strained. Unlike Amanda, Holly was still in the dreaming stage and wasn't ready to make any big moves; she just wanted to vent her frustrations without receiving any guidance.

Amanda and I were working together when this unfolded, and I encouraged her to stay focused on her own journey if she wanted her friendship with Holly to survive. The truth was, no matter how much Amanda wanted to help, Holly needed to be able to make her own choice. Amanda's intentions were noble, but her execution was pushing her friend away and straining their relationship.

While Holly struggled along, Amanda carved out a new life for herself and her family. She had joys and struggles unique to her situation as an entrepreneur with a husband and three children. Holly, on the other hand, was a single woman who was still teaching, trying to determine the appropriate timing for when she could leave the classroom, if ever. She was doing the best she could with the beliefs she had.

Like Amanda and Holly, each of us has a unique threshold for how much risk we are willing to take, including you. We all must make choices and changes in our own time. You've seen this in your own life, I'm assuming, whether you succeeded or not. It is completely normal to make a choice, receive feedback, weigh out the pros and cons, and then make another choice. Eventually, you find what best serves you when you are ready.

As you move forward in your life, remember your pace and evolution will be different from others, so you mustn't compare. Please, don't compare pants. Your best friend may take huge risks that make you sick to your stomach when you consider applying them to your life, or you might judge a sibling who complains endlessly about his or her unhappiness (but fails to act).

It's so important to lead by example and stay away from comparison.

Transitions are challenging enough without trying to walk down someone else's path. Leave other people to make their own, unique choices and use all your energy to rock yours.

HOW TO PUT YOUR BIG GIRL PANTS ON

DO NOT COMPARE PANTS

Remember, judging others for their choices does nothing for you except show you the things you want to change about yourself. What bothers you in someone else is likely something that bothers you about you, too.

List three things that bug you about other people.

Now turn them around on yourself.

Once you begin noticing these faults and insecurities, it's easier to work toward fixing them.

Write down three things you can do differently today, to help you overcome your frustrations:

CHAPTER 7:

BOUNDARIES ARE BRILLIANT

No is a complete sentence.

-Anne Lamott

Women notoriously say yes to every task or favor asked of them to avoid disappointing or hurting people. Often, the yes mentality stems from a subconscious desire to meet societal standards as the nurturing, helpful sex we're supposed to be. As we discussed all the way back in chapter one, this can be the difference between acting as your authentic self and your social self. It's easy to see these issues and acknowledge them, but when I redirect the question to you, it may be harder to accept. So, to ease in, we'll talk about other women for a bit before I shift the focus to you.

Think about the difference between men and women when it comes to saying yes and no. Do more of the men you know find it easy or hard to say no? Now, think about this:

How often do women say yes to things they don't want to do? And, in doing that, how often are they saying no to something else they'd rather be doing?

Yes, I will pick up the doughnuts on the way to work. I can't sleep in for the extra 15 minutes I truly need.

Yes, I will host a baby shower for you. Even though I'm struggling with my own infertility.

Yes, I will fill in for you at the board meeting tomorrow night. And miss my son's soccer game for the second time this month.

What women are missing when they constantly put others before themselves is critical to every person's mental well-being. If people don't know your boundaries, they won't know you are overwhelmed until it's too late.

Personal boundaries are the physical, emotional, and mental limits we use to protect ourselves from being manipulated or used by other people, and they are exactly what more women need in their lives. A boundary is like a property line, allowing the creator of the boundary to separate themselves—who they are, how they feel, and what they think—from the thoughts and feelings of other people. With clear boundaries in place, a person can create and keep an understanding of where they are, what they believe, and where someone else's desires begin. This is critical to creating and maintaining personal space.

So now let's talk about you:

When you feel anger or resentment building, your body is telling you it's time to create a boundary. And don't freak out, learning to set boundaries takes time. There will be some discomfort as you move forward, but facing and working through this discomfort is what will ultimately lead to massive personal reward.

When used appropriately, personal boundaries:

- Help determine responsibilities
- Show you who you are
- Allow you to respect and nurture yourself so you can be of service to other people when it's appropriate.

Awesome!

But is there a way to learn to say no? Is it possible to build a backbone and stand up for yourself without being too passive or too argumentative? Finding the balance is key. You can do that in four easy steps.

Step One: Identify the issue and how it makes you feel

To learn how to build and respect your own boundaries, you first need to identify the overlooked issues that make you feel overworked and underappreciated. Each time someone asks you to complete a task, it's important to consider how it makes you feel and why it makes you feel that way. Of course, this must be done before you make a choice.

For example, when my kids were younger, I sometimes felt great about volunteering at school. Other times I felt it stretched me too thin. Occasionally contributing made me feel connected, happy and involved in my kids' growth and development, but getting too involved made me feel as if I couldn't get my own work done during the day. So why did I find myself going to school more than I was comfortable?

I felt guilty knowing others were in the classroom all the time, so I began showing up and overextending myself. And I became exhausted because of it.

Step Two: Talk it Out

When women consider voicing their concerns, it's not uncommon for them to fear being disliked if they disagree with someone or have to tell them no. A good way to overcome this fear is by practicing or talking out the problem with someone else before making any specific decisions. Hashing out the pros and cons of each choice, with a friend or coach, will help give you the confidence you need to set your boundary.

I have a friend who is a great listener, and we function as sounding boards for one another. We talk about what is bothering us and how much time and energy—if any—we can give to other people. The goal of our conversations is always the same: to connect and talk so we can keep each other sane.

We make sure to keep each other focused on our own limits and not the feelings or reactions of others. We ask one another a couple of questions:

- What can we put up with?
- Are our feelings of guilt stemming from worrying about trying to please someone else?

Step Three: Speak Up

Once you know what you need to do, you must take the next, and quite possibly the hardest, step and speak directly to the person (or people) asking you to do whatever it is you don't want to. Be prepared to stand firm in your decision when and if you are asked to reconsider. That is the entire point of setting boundaries. This does not mean you must be aggressive or angry. Quite the opposite. It's possible to stay neutral, clear, gracious, and direct.

Step Four: Follow Through

Simply, do what you said you would do. Not only is this important to keep yourself sane, but it will also help others respect your boundaries, giving you credibility and building your integrity.

Building boundaries might feel uncomfortable at first, but they are vital if you are going to maintain a sense of self. This is not a power play or an attention-seeking move. Instead, it's a way to minimize outside distractions that keep you from pursuing your life's purpose. Through carving out time and space for you, you can design a life that fits you perfectly.

While we've dissected how to set your own boundaries, there might be a few other concerns you have before mastering your boundary-making skills. Keep these thoughts in mind as you move forward:

- You are not responsible for how someone reacts to your boundaries. If someone is upset, it is his/her problem.
- You might feel selfish or guilty at first, but you will be empowered and confident with practice.
- Remain firm when someone challenges your boundary; he or she might be used to hearing "yes" all the time.

- The driving force behind boundaries is desire. If there's a good reason for a boundary, stay motivated to maintain it.

REAL WOMEN'S WOES

Becky

Becky went into business for herself after a friend offered to be her first paying client. She was going to be a writer, taking on ghostwriting, editing, and copywriting for clients. Becky loved the work around words and didn't want to restrict her creativity to one of those avenues, so she felt comfortable offering all those services.

During her first month in business, Becky's friend, Amy, referred many of her own clients to Becky. It was incredibly appreciated and helpful, and Becky was convinced she'd made the right choice leaving her 9-5 job behind.

As the months passed and her clientele grew, Becky noticed that Amy began getting frustrated when Becky's schedule wasn't open for her work. Amy would lash out and demand that Becky push another client's deadline back, even when she knew she was asking for a quick, sometimes unrealistic, turn around.

Can you see where this is going?

Becky felt somewhat obligated to take Amy's work because she was thankful Amy helped her build her career, but Becky also knew that pushing other people aside to do her friend's work would look bad and rub her clients wrong. She didn't want to lose them while trying to appease Amy.

Becky and I discussed the pros and cons of doing her business both ways: taking on Amy's work as a priority and taking Amy's work as she would any other clients'. Becky told me she'd feel better if Amy played by the rules like everyone else, so we role played the conversation Becky would have with Amy when the time came and the issue popped up again.

After Becky set her boundary with Amy, Amy continued to work with her. There were times when she tried to test Becky and see if she would give her preferential treatment, but Becky held strong in her resolve to treat Amy as she would any other client.

This boundary, though seemingly difficult at first, allowed Becky to give as much time to her other clients, causing them to feel appreciated, valued and respected. Had Becky continued treating Amy more importantly, it's possible Becky could've lost several of her clients and her income. After the conversation, Becky felt empowered and in control of her business. She knew she was earning money because the work she was doing was valuable, not because her friend was funneling her business as a favor.

HOW TO PUT YOUR BIG GIRL PANTS ON

BOUNDARIES ARE BEAUTIFUL

Let's identify some areas in your life where you'd like to create or strengthen your personal boundaries.

I'd like to strengthen my boundaries around my finances by:

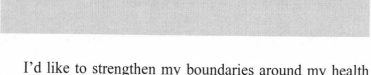

I'd like to strengthen my boundaries around my health by:

I'd like to strengthen my boundaries around my relationships by:

I'd like to strengthen my boundaries around my career by:

Now, choose one of the boundaries from above and focus on it for a full week. Plan to make changes throughout the week, consciously considering each decision you make and committing to sharing that boundary with others who question it.

CHAPTER 8:

KEEP MOVING FORWARD

It always seems impossible until it's done.

-Nelson Mandela

In my twenties, I went on a three-week trip to Australia. At the time, I was ungrateful, upset this expedition was cutting into my social schedule. My parents sent me with a group of people I didn't know because they thought it would be a great experience. I suspected it would be a total drag (but didn't see how big of a drag I was being).

While traveling around the country, one of our stops was the Great Barrier Reef. The only certified scuba diver in the group, I considered not going out on an excursion because I didn't want to go alone. However, I knew my chances of returning to Queensland were slim, so I decided the opportunity to dive there was more significant than my fear, so I went for it.

Once on the boat, I realized nobody else spoke English besides me, and I'd been paired off with a dive buddy (this is a standard safety precaution) who couldn't understand a word I said, even when I told him, "I will not go into any caves."

Holding my mask in place with one hand and knowing it was too late to turn back, I rolled off the back of the boat into the water, certain my dive partner had no clue how terrified I was.

Ten minutes into our dive, we swam toward a wide opening of what appeared to be a cave. *Oh God, please no, I thought. Please don't let this be a cave. Please don't let us go inside.*

Sure enough, despite the fact I signaled an emphatic no, my dive buddy proceeded into the abyss with the rest of the group. I had no other option but to go in too, considering I didn't want to be left for dead at the bottom of the south seas.

I could feel the pounding of my heart through my regulator. I was in full panic mode, convinced I was going to die. I kept trying to regulate my buoyancy so my tank would stop scraping the top of the cave, but I couldn't focus on anything other than living through this.

At one point, I was breathing so heavily I started flipping out about my air supply. *Was I going to use up all my oxygen and perish right there? What if I need to buddy breathe? Did I even pass this portion of the dive test? I don't even remember how to share a regulator. Holy shit.* The more I panicked, the heavier I breathed. The heavier I breathed, the more I panicked. I knew I had to stop freaking out and get ahold of myself, so I slowed my breath down, concentrating on each inhale and exhale. Somehow—by the grace of God—focusing on the rhythm of my breath calmed me down. As my breaths slowed, so did my thoughts.

Maybe I can do this.

Maybe I am not going to die.

This is actually pretty amazing.

How many people get to do something like this in their lifetime?

I'm so fortunate.

I'm glad I'm here.

Just like that, I transitioned from wondering who would miss me when I died, to slowly noticing the life - the sea urchins - living in the cracks and crevices of the cave walls. My whole thought shift was purely magical. Swimming along, I started to feel a sense of calm.

When we came out the other side, I was in a whole new underwater world, surrounded by the most electrifyingly colorful fish and flora I have ever seen. For a moment, I didn't have a care in the world. For the first time in my life, I was fully present, without runaway thoughts or worries.

The day before and the day after didn't matter; amongst the ocean's beautiful creatures, I felt like I was floating in pure, uninhibited peace.

Looking back now, I know why I panicked. I planted the seed of doubt before I submerged into the sea. I had closed myself off to the opportunity before I even started the dive. I said no before considering a yes.

Had I stuck with my original refusal, I never would've had the amazing dive experience I now consider a cherished memory and a life-changing experience.

I am convinced my dive in the Great Barrier Reef paved the way for the courageous moments I have needed throughout my adult life because I had to learn—quickly— nothing amazing comes from being comfortable. I had to feel fear, face it, and decide on my next move. The cave started as a metaphor for my own life but has transformed into one for how and why I coach others.

How many times a day do you stop before you begin? How often do your stories stop you from living fully?

You must enter and swim through your own cave if you ever want to experience the pure beauty, fulfillment, and joy awaiting you on the other side. Although you will never know what the other side looks or feels like until it's reached, embarking on the journey is the most important, critical part of the process.

If you want to grow, expand, and explore all life has to offer, there are no other options but to just go in, go through, and come out the other side. You can, you should, and when you're brave enough, you will.

REAL WOMEN'S WOES

Betsy

Betsy was on the road to a prescription-drug addiction. After her knee surgery, she was sent home with enough Oxycodone to get her through the worst of her pain. But, enough wasn't enough for Betsy. She *needed* more.

The physical relief she was getting from the medication was also relieving the emotional pain she carried from the pressure she felt to excel in college and on the athletic field. She refilled her prescription, not once, but twice, and when her doctor would no longer prescribe her more, she started conjuring up different ailments, going from urgent care to urgent care, always convincing the physicians her new malady called for hardcore meds.

Suzanne

Suzanne lost her daughter after seven months in the womb. She grieved her loss silently, as people encouraged her to move on with her life. Nobody understood why it was important for Suzanne to remember and talk about her baby, and they judged her unfairly for it, wondering why she couldn't simply move on and try to get pregnant again. She'd heard a lot of people miscarry babies from many of her friends, and she logically knew this to be true, but after several years of coping and trying to heal, Suzanne still couldn't bring herself to try for another baby.

Becca

Becca stopped making art after her first show was a total flop. She stayed in her safe and tedious corporate position, deciding she'd have to learn how to live life without pursuing her lifelong dream. Secretly, Becca kept the studio set up in her apartment and pulled out the oil pastels when she'd suffered a particularly hard day, but she never shared her work with others and threw away her canvas paintings when she was done. One failure ruined her love of art.

All three women, all with different obstacles to face, had one thing in common - they all *felt* the same: embarrassed, guilty, hurt, and afraid. Their lives had taken unexpected turns and they didn't know what to do next. Instead of going in, going through, and coming out the other side, they began to swim around in their stories and focus their energies on the *what ifs*.

What if Betsy couldn't find a way to deal with her stress other than with drugs? What if her parents were disappointed in her? What if she went to rehab but went right back to drugs after?

What if people were talking behind Suzanne's back, judging her? What if she never got over the heartbreak and humiliation? What if she was unworthy and never able to carry a baby to full term? Was she to blame for her loss?

What if Becca's friends and family never realized how lonely she was without her art? What if she decided to never paint again? How would she feel without her vivid, emotional masterpieces that helped manage her stress?

Doubt is common. Seriously, as women, we are way too hard on ourselves, denying our strength and looking for reasons we can't move forward. As a result, we end up spending many of life's precious moments basking in our self-imposed prisons of fear.

Yet, just because this type of behavior is common for women, doesn't mean it has to be common for you. So, how can you move forward, overcoming obstacles and creating a vibrant, happy life?

Stop running from your stories and truths. Yes, you will feel vulnerable and exposed, and every unknown you face will be terrifying (or induce some level of fear and resistance in you). But when that fear creeps up and you want to turn around and run away, consider the reason the rearview mirror is so small and the windshield is so big: where you're headed is much more beautiful than where you've been.

Look through the windshield at the road ahead and get ready to plan your next move.

HOW TO PUT YOUR BIG GIRL PANTS ON

PLAN

Up until now, we've talked about overcoming fears by facing them head on, but goal setting can help you eliminate long-standing, seemingly insurmountable fears.

What is one fear you haven't faced (but know facing it would help you move forward and reach goals)?

Map your Moves:

- On fresh paper, write down an idea (whether personal or business related) on the center of the paper and circle it. (For example, I want to do stand-up comedy, take a vacation, or learn how to garden.)
- Draw lines outward from the circled word or phrase, and then, at the end of each line, write some more words associated with the ideas you

have about the goal in the middle. (If following the comedy example, your words could include amateur night, writing a sketch, making a video for YouTube.)

- Continue branching out and getting more specific, adding multiple branches to each concept if necessary.
- Once you're finished, number them in the order in which you'd like to tackle them.

CHAPTER 9:

NEVER STOP

If you don't go after what you want, you'll never have it.
If you don't ask, the answer will always be no.
If you don't step forward, you're always in the same place.

-Nora Roberts

Though the phrase "they put their pants on one leg at a time" is often used to tell us we all put on our pants the same way (so we are equal and comparison shouldn't happen), I think there's a practical side to it that seems so obvious, we rarely talk about it. Yet, it's often overlooked.

One leg, one step, or one action is the answer to all feelings of stagnation.

Whether you know where you're going or you feel stuck, the answer to "what should I do next?" is always going to be to take some sort of action. We know we want to be happy, but what is required?

It's simple: People don't become happy by simply deciding to be. They act. It's an important component of the process and why I had you map out your goals in the last chapter, but it is not the only factor. In my own life, I must acknowledge I don't end up dressed because I decide I want to be dressed. I end up with clothes on when I act.

You need to take action; put your legs into your pants, pull 'em up and button yourself in.

Putting on pants is such a great metaphor for all these risky-sounding life changes. It feels familiar and easy. It's not a trick; action steps do not need to be big, bold, or scary. You may take almost indiscernible action now, but it is not to be ignored. It's highly possible your choice to live differently means you are the only one who actually notices. Your action may be to wake up 30 minutes earlier each day, cut out soda, start to write love letters to your partner again, or take a cleansing breath before you speak. It's less important what the action step is and more important that you are aware of strategically making moves to do things differently.

Ultimately, your action steps are the key to taking control of your life. Yes, your thoughts inspire those actions, but thoughts alone will not deliver the future you want (nor will a well-planned map).

In the absence of action

If you're not sold on making a change, big or small, know the outcome is predictable. You will experience the mind-numbing sameness you have always endured. Tomorrow will feel the same as today and I can bet your semi-enthusiastic outlook on your career, marriage, friendship, or project will remain completely intact. But you'll know this routine, so you'll feel safe. It's both suffocating and reassuring to think about.

Safe job? No pressure to leave. Cheating spouse? You know what to expect. Judgmental friends? At least they look good in group photos.

If you feel unfulfilled right now, imagine how you'll feel in a year or two. Imagine life when you don't make changes and you've survived two more years of mediocrity. While you might not feel a sense of urgency, and there truly might not be one, you will always remain stuck unless you actively pursue that fresh start with an engaging job, a new love interest or supportive friends.

Of course, there are times when staying the same isn't bad, so please don't misunderstand my commentary. Remaining stationary is only a bummer if you're not a fan of what you currently have in your life. If you're completely 100% satisfied with every area of your life, then it's okay to want more of your days to match. However, sameness is a soul-killer when you know deep, deep down you want something different.

If you want something different, you must do something different. Step into your new reality and stop wasting time. Your time on Earth is finite and can pass quickly if you stay busy with things that don't support your purpose. Don't block yourself from your dreams with seemingly noble pursuits that fill too much time in your day. These can force you to stay still. If dutifully attending to your marriage, children, household chores, career, friends, or other responsibilities has proven to suck fulfillment from your life, something has to change.

When you come to the point in your life when you take stock of your journey's progress, it may feel late in the game. It's natural to feel overwhelmed or panicked; there is still so much you want to do and not a ton of time left to do it.

Let this sense of urgency motivate you to act in a way you've never been pressured to do before!

Your only option is to take steps in the direction of your dreams as soon as you feel called to action. If you worry about needing more motivation than the speedy passage of time, consider the telling questions:

How will you feel at this time next year if you do not take an action step toward your dream?

What if everything remains the same?

Don't wait until next year to find out.

REAL WOMEN'S WOES

Kate

Kate was my first client. She heard about me through a friend of a friend and hired me after our first introductory call. Our first in-person meeting took place at Starbucks. After we said our hellos, she wanted to get down to business, handing me a diet plan and telling me she wanted to lose 50 pounds.

From across the table, Kate looked at me matter-of-factly while the rest of the coffee shop bustled with busy people behind us.

"Should I even be using coffee creamer? Isn't it pretty fattening?" She laughed, waiting for me to respond.

Because I was still somewhat insecure about my coaching career, my first inclination was to pretend I was an expert on the calories in milk products. Yet, I had promised myself to always be authentic after years of hiding away or pretending to be someone else. I gently placed my hands on the table between us, looked her in the eyes and said, "I ate Oreos for breakfast today. I have no idea if you should put cream in your coffee." We both laughed, though Kate appeared somewhat surprised. I thought it might be because she signed up for a package without knowing what she'd get from it, but I couldn't project that insecurity onto her. All I could do was coach from my zone of genius and hold space for her to figure out who she was and how she wanted to show up.

From there, a beautiful coach/client relationship was born. We didn't talk about caloric intake; we talked about what was going on in her life. Turns out, most of her life, her father made her feel badly about herself. What she craved wasn't a cookie. She wanted to feel love, acceptance, support, and belonging. Her problem wasn't her weight. It never really was. Eventually, Kate lost her 50 pounds, and the thing is, we never, ever talked about food (besides those Oreos).

She realized it was time to make the shift, and so she did. It was a natural next step for a woman who wanted to live lighter and be lighter. Her heart said, "it's time" and she listened.

Kate knew it was her moment to step into her life. Her decision and readiness to make a change were the biggest, hardest and most powerful steps she took. In declaring her intention to change, even without knowing what she needed to do, Kate took back her life by committing to doing the work required. The outcome? Her best, most vibrant self. Kate knew the journey toward happiness would take time, but she constantly showed up and listened to the voice telling her to take one small step at a time, one after the next in the direction of her future.

Amazing, isn't she?

These real-life stories I've shared throughout the book highlight the successes I've seen in my practice, along with some of the people who've stayed stuck. Yes, they felt grief, guilt, or shame and they struggled, but what is the difference between them? Is there some big secret between the ones who made it to the other side successfully while others stayed stuck?

No.

You are just like Kate, Lindsey, and Suzanne. Becca, too. They all made the best choices they knew how. The only difference between the women who succeeded in moving forward and those who remained still in their lives was the choice to find a better way and then execute. To take those baby steps and trust they would lead their dreams into becoming realities.

In that way, you are just like them, too.

You can have it all.

HOW TO PUT YOUR BIG GIRL PANTS ON

NEVER STOP

Here's the accountability piece. Write down three ways you took your mapped actions from (Chapter 8) and stepped toward them. Don't worry if you haven't done anything yet (and you're reading straight through); this is where you'll write down your actions as you progress through the next week.

Why do you have to do these things now?

Why is this your time to make a change?

CONCLUSION

Be the silent watcher of your thoughts and behavior.
You are beneath the thinker. You are the stillness beneath
the mental noise. You are the love and joy beneath the pain.

-Eckhart Tolle

Ready to pull up and rock out your pants? It's go time!

I've given you a lot of steps to take you to this moment, and we've talked about some critical pieces to make sure you don't fail along the way. Pulling up and putting on your big girl pants might seem overwhelmingly different than the way you've lived your life until now, but I can assure you, practicing each step will make it seem less and less difficult.

Ready to break down and bundle together everything we've learned?

Let's do it.

At this point, you should understand—at the very least—whether what you currently have is what you want. You have tools to figure out what it is you truly want (and how you want to feel), how to articulate your dream to the people in your life, how to build healthy boundaries so you can take care of yourself while you transform, and how to set and step toward goals that will—eventually—lead you to the life you want.

In truth, you've always had both the knowledge and wisdom to get to this point, but sometimes it's hard to see our own problems when they are so, so close to us. Even though you might know the answer to your most challenging issue, how many times have you sought out advice and insight from someone else you thought had everything figured out? Maybe they appear to be navigating through life without struggle.

The truth is, silence and introspection can give you as much knowledge as those you consider sage. Your mind whispers encouragement and impassioned knowledge each time you take steps toward the things you want and need in life. It peeks out of your subconscious as you ask yet another friend for her opinion. It lays with you as you fret, cry, and wonder at 3:00 am, sleepless in bed and uncomfortable in uncertainty.

You, my friend, are wise. And your wisdom aches to guide you.

Your soul swells with hope to share its vision with you.

Putting on your big girl pants is remembering the beautiful power you have to be yourself. You get to choose the life you experience. Isn't that incredible? But what's more incredible is the truth of it all, the fact that women so often overlook because we're told to be submissive, subservient or friendly, without making anyone uncomfortable (besides ourselves):

- You've had the power all along
- Now is the time to pull up those pants and wear your power with authority
- When in doubt, read this letter to your future self and remember your worth.

Dear Future Me,

I've seen you. You've been strutting around like you know your worth. I don't know what it is about you, but something just seems different, powerful and new. I used to know what to expect. But now? You are this new version of us and it's a little shocking.

Don't get me wrong, I like it. I'm not used to seeing you stand your ground or act on your ideas so quickly. It is refreshing to see someone who is confident. It's almost like you're somehow bigger now. Not your butt or anything, but your whole presence just seems...bigger.

I'm not sure what you have planned next, but I'm excited to see what you come up with. Watching you makes me so proud. You're finally doing all the things you used to secretly daydream about. You have stepped into a reality I never knew existed. It's falling into place with perfect timing.

Rock on!
Sincerely,
Your former self.

Can you do it?

Unquestionably, yes.

THANK YOU!

I hope you realize you can have anything you desire if you simply do one thing: step into your power. You are kick ass. You know this now, right?

Just in case you need another reminder before you go forth and conquer:

- All the fears you hold are only as big as you allow them to be
- You deserve all the happiness you want
- You are worthy of a life you crave, one that makes you feel like the courageous champion you are.

Take the steps outlined here and apply them to every area of life you'd like to improve. Day by day, minute by minute, you'll feel even more empowered and amazing than you do in this moment.

If at any point you need a boost, a pep-talk, or a hand, or if you're making changes that seem too good to be true, I am here to guide you through your journey!

Readers, I'd love to hear from you. Stop by my website and leave me a note about the pieces of this book that truly resonate with you. While you're digging around, sign up to be in a drawing for a free VIP coaching session.

If you know someone who could use help in finding and wearing her own pants, tell them about your experience with this book so they, too, can start their transformational journey. It's reassuring to have the support of others as you step into your new life.

I'd love to hear from you:
www.lisapanos.com
lisa@lisapanos.com
Facebook: www.facebook.com/lisabairdpanos
Instagram: lisapanos4700
Twitter: twitter.com/panoslisa

This is my life....my story....my book.
I will no longer let anyone else write it;
nor will I apologize for the edits I make.
—Steve Maraboli

48161894R00085

Made in the USA
San Bernardino, CA
18 April 2017